Pebble™ Plus

Bugs, Bugs, Bugs!

Bumble Bees

by Fran Howard

Consulting Editor: Gail Saunders-Smith, PhD

Consultant: Gary A. Dunn, MS, Director of Education
Young Entomologists' Society Inc.
Lansing, Michigan

Capstone
press

Mankato, Minnesota

Pebble Plus is published by Capstone Press,
151 Good Counsel Drive, P.O. Box 669, Mankato, Minnesota 56002.
www.capstonepress.com

1 2 3 4 5 6 10 09 08 07 06 05

Library of Congress Cataloging-in-Publication Data
Howard, Fran, 1953–
    Bumble bees/by Fran Howard.
    p. cm.—(Pebble plus: bugs, bugs, bugs!)
    Includes bibliographical references and index.
    ISBN 0-7368-3642-X (hardcover)
    1. Bumble bees—Juvenile literature. I. Title. II. Series.
QL568.A6H59 2005
595.79'9—dc22   2004011969

Summary: Simple text and photographs describe the physical characteristics of bumble bees.

Editorial Credits
Sarah L. Schuette, editor; Linda Clavel, set designer; Kate Opseth, book designer; Kelly Garvin,
    photo researcher; Scott Thoms, photo editor

Photo Credits
Bruce Coleman Inc./E.R. Degginger, 13; J.C. Carton, 9; Kim Taylor, cover, 18–19; Larry West, 10–11
Color-Pic Inc./Phil Degginger, 5
Digital Vision/Gerry Willis and Michael Durham, 1
Dwight R. Kuhn, 14–15, 17
McDonald Wildlife Photography/Joe McDonald, 6–7
Photodisc, back cover
Robert McCaw, 21

Note to Parents and Teachers

The Bugs, Bugs, Bugs! set supports national science standards related to the diversity of
life and heredity. This book describes and illustrates bumble bees. The images support
early readers in understanding the text. The repetition of words and phrases helps early
readers learn new words. This book also introduces early readers to subject-specific
vocabulary words, which are defined in the Glossary section. Early readers may need
assistance to read some words and to use the Table of Contents, Glossary, Read More,
Internet Sites, and Index sections of the book.

Table of Contents

What Are Bumble Bees?

Bumble bees are insects
with round, hairy bodies.
Bumble bees buzz.

How Bumble Bees Look

Most bumble bees are
black, yellow, or orange.
They have thin wings.

Bumble bees are about
the size of a jelly bean.

9

Bumble bees have
two antennas. Bumble bees
use their antennas to smell,
feel, and hear.

Bumble bees have five eyes.

Two eyes are big.

Three eyes are small.

What Bumble Bees Do

Bumble bees live
in nests in the ground.
A queen bumble bee
makes a new nest each year.

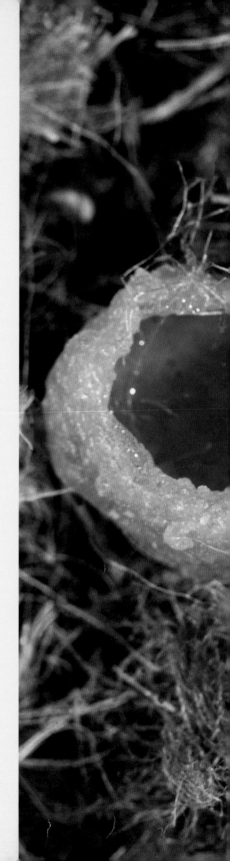

Bumble bees drink
nectar from flowers.
Nectar gives bumble bees
energy to fly.

Bumble bees fly
back to the nest.
They bring nectar back
for young bumble bees
to eat.

Bumble bees collect
pollen from flowers.
Bumble bees help
new flowers and crops grow.

21

Glossary

antenna—a feeler; insects use antennas to sense movement, to smell, and to listen to each other.

energy—the ability to do work

insect—a small animal with a hard outer shell, six legs, three body sections, and two antennas; most insects have wings.

nectar—a sweet liquid found in flowers

nest—a home built by an animal to lay eggs and raise their young; about 200 bumble bees can live in one nest.

pollen—the tiny, yellow grains in flowers; pollen helps plants produce seeds.

Read More

Birch, Robin. *Bees Up Close.* Minibeasts Up Close. Chicago: Raintree, 2004.

Tagliaferro, Linda. *Bees and Their Hives.* Animal Homes. Mankato, Minn.: Capstone Press, Pebble Plus, 2004.

Trumbauer, Lisa. *The Life Cycle of a Bee.* Life Cycles. Mankato, Minn.: Pebble Books, 2003.

Internet Sites

FactHound offers a safe, fun way to find Internet sites related to this book. All of the sites on FactHound have been researched by our staff.

Here's how:

1. Visit *www.facthound.com*

2. Type in this special code **073683642X** for age-appropriate sites. Or enter a search word related to this book for a more general search.

3. Click on the **Fetch It** button.

FactHound will fetch the best sites for you!

Index

Word Count: 123
Grade: 1
Early-Intervention Level: 9

24